Matter's Music

—Researches—

(A Vienna Notebook)

Paul Kelley

BuschekBooks
Ottawa

Library and Archives Canada Cataloguing in Publication

Kelley, Paul, 1951-
Matter's music/researches : (a Vienna notebook) / Paul Kelley.

ISBN 978-1-894543-65-1

I. Title.

PS8621.E43M38 2010 C818'.6 C2010-905836-4

Cover background image: Sandstone, textured, wall background, istockphoto
File #: 6157002

Printed in Winnipeg, Manitoba, by Hignell Book Printing.

BuschekBooks, P.O. Box 74053, 5 Beechwood Avenue
Ottawa, Ontario, Canada K1M 2H9
www.buschekbooks.com

BuschekBooks gratefully acknowledges the support of the Canada Council for
the Arts for its publishing program.

**Canada Council
for the Arts**

**Conseil des Arts
du Canada**

for Susan

Conternts

"... to hearken to the sounds of the day as if they were the chords of eternity."
—Karl Kraus

Once upon a time in Vienna. . .

1.

«. . . from one light into another.»
("Letters to Felician")

Upon returning to a foreign city where one has known many pleasant, if not
  joyous, moments in the past, one wants immediately to return to
  the favourite places, to return even to the routes that lead to those
  places and connect them. With one's feet and eyes, with one's whole
  body, one wants not only a confirmation of memory; one wants to
  join memory with physical substance—buildings, squares, parks,
  fragrances, sounds—, to make memory come alive. In this way, the
  boundaries that separate memory from actuality, past from present,
  reality from reverie do not dissolve but become porous. From this
  moment on, the visitor who returns to his or her past is henceforth
  doubled, as familiar and as strange as is the city itself. Everywhere, two
  posthumous existences encounter each other.

Tourists are always of the very sights they go to see, inextricable from the
  spectacles they have travelled so far to behold and in which they act
  their allotted roles of strolling, looking, eating, drinking, talking,
  laughing, listening—all of which they now *perform*, as they cannot be
  "performed" in the normal setting of their everyday lives.

What if the man at the table facing mine on the terrace of this café is merely
  pretending to be talking to someone on his cell-phone? Because he is
  wearing wrap-around sunglasses, this suspicion has possibilities. For
  speech, even on a telephone, is as much a matter of eyes as of voice.

I count no fewer than three people writing in their notebooks at this café.
  (Vienna is a writerly city.) Were I to take out this notebook and begin
  to write in it (perhaps about the writers at their notebooks—one
  young man and two young women), I would make the "fourth" in a
  game we would all be playing differently.

A sudden rain shower has brought an end to the music that has been blasting from the street just below the corner windows (part of the Street Festival that has been scheduled, in part to coincide with the Euro-Cup Soccer matches, for every weekend of this month). Here is a welcome reprieve. I thank this rain. A quiet has been turned on.

The steady, assertive clack of her shoes on the paving stones: everyone on the terrace turns in her direction as she walks by; but they do not turn at once. —But what if they did all turn at once?

The flutter of the white curtain at the window billowing *over* the street, adorning it with all one can imagine of the entanglements, the reachings, the surrenders of the apartment's inhabitants: their story is inscribed in white words on that curtain for all to behold and be awed.

Owing to the rain, the Café Anzengruber across the street from the flat where I am staying has permitted several of the performers from the street festival to play and sing for the diners and drinkers. (I am eating goulasch and drinking a smooth red wine.) Most of them are poor; all are loud. One just sang a version of Johnny Cash's "Ring Of Fire" in German—an experience (if that's what it was) I will never be allowed to forget!

2.

Late last night I met T.K., the man who will be my flat-mate for the next several
days. Although we "met" each other, we did not actually see each
other, for we turned on no light but rather sat at the table in the dark
room talking animatedly about all manner of things and drinking wine
until the early morning hours. Our conversation, desultory and intense
at once (in the dark, one listens better: the life of the words is not
separable from the intimacy of the speaker's voice), must be counted
among the best I have ever enjoyed.

I think: yes, there may still be hope.

Elderly people do not talk on their cell-phones in public. For this, we should
earnestly thank them.

Rare to see an elderly person sitting alone at a sidewalk café. Cafés are for
talking, looking, listening in the present, a present in which an elderly
person becomes *more* vulnerable, *more* frail, *more* alone—unable to be
recalled by his/her memories. In a busy café full of young people, the
elderly person would experience a sense of having been abandoned
by his/her life to the tune of all the chatter which erects walls without
doors or windows.

The young woman on the street corner facing mine, talking on her cell-phone.
She ends her conversation just as the walk sign signals her to move to
the corner opposite. As she crosses to the new corner, she is already
pushing buttons on the cell-phone, which she holds up before her
face. When she reaches the new corner, she begins a new conversation,
standing there, stock-still, as on the previous corner, while other
pedestrians walk around her. I imagine her crossing to all the corners
in just this fashion, north, south, east, and west—circling—until there
is no one left for her to phone. Gradually, she fades away until she
disappears entirely. Only her cell-phone is left behind, on the sidewalk,
where a young man in baggy pants and running shoes picks it up.
Looking around to ensure that its owner is nowhere in sight, he starts
to push its buttons as he crosses the street. . . .

In the square below: the sounds of a fight made of small dogs.

Shouldn't someone be sitting in the eight empty chairs grouped around the table
in this room? I feel as if I am waiting for guests to arrive and a party to
begin. (My nervousness.)

"These androgynous hours."

Philosophy might experience some needed salutary changes if its current
practitioners were to "do" it, i.e., enter into conversations, by sitting in
the dark in their underwear.

The truism has it that the traveller is dislodged from time—detemporalized—as
much as from space. But it is also true that the traveller is claimed by
the time and the place from which he or she is separated. At 7.00 am,
I said to myself, "It's only 1.00 am in my home; there S. and K. are still
sleeping soundly and warmly in their beds."—To be, if only briefly,
in two times and two places at once: that is the true experience of
detemporalization and despatialization. In that experience, at once
anomalous and anachronous, the traveller makes a fragile home.

3.

All the happy liquids in their contented containers.

He chose to smoke cigarettes lighter in nicotine and tar than the brand he usually
smoked, but he smoked twice as many of them. So much for "healthful"
decisions.

In the early morning, the songs of the birds are isolated, as if each were no more
than a simple statement. Then the traffic noises start, but they, too,
sound isolated: one car, one truck, one motorcycle at a time, each in its
own moment, declaring itself.

This will be a light-headed day: something surely breezy is going on in the
crowns of those ash trees.

The squeaking of the chair when I sit down in it or change my position—it is
somehow reassuring to me. (Until now, I was not aware that I was in
need of reassuring.)

I find myself talking to myself in a very low voice, almost a whisper, as if, by
speaking more loudly, I might disturb the objects in this flat.

Now that the clouds have arrived, I am better able to concentrate.

The sound of bottles clattering—*many* bottles clattering—as if being delivered
or collected, punctuated by the almost inaudible cry of a tiny baby.

What would three-and-a-half-year-old K. most enjoy here? All the stairs and
staircases, of course! —And the thick beams and bridgework in the
attic, the dust motes circling, rising, and falling in rays of light admitted
through the thick glass of the narrow windows.

The syncopated rhythms of the windows banging in the wind: clamour and
music at once.

Like me, the sun is unable to stay out and unable to stay in. The sun, the clouds,
and I: what a mess we're in.

What if the clanging of bottles continued, with only very brief interruptions, all
day and all night long? Perhaps the silences would then become the
more annoying in as much as they would not permit to the sound of
the jostling glass the constancy it would need to attain a state of easy
ignorability, such as that which cushions or makes inaudible almost
any other annoying urban sound.

I return to the flat from the Naschmarkt and the shops weighted with
provisions—apples, strawberries, bread rolls, peppers, tomatoes,
potatoes, sheep's cheese, ham, sausages, mustard, horseradish,
mayonnaise, beer and wine. I unpack them and put them away. Having
accomplished such an important task, I sit down, contented, and open
a beer, which I drink in the spirit of one who, because relieved of the
pressures of necessity, can now afford to be open to whatever might
come this way, one who has the freedom to have a future.

The workers from the restaurant's kitchen are smoking cigarettes and laughing
quietly in a doorway less than ten meters down the street from its
awninged entrance. To the patrons of the restaurant, even as they pass
them to enter it, the workers laughing and talking quietly in their food-
stained white aprons and uniforms, are invisible and inaudible.

Memory is free from any obligation or command, free even from the expectation
to be useful. Just this freedom brings any person's memories near
to the realm of art (though obviously without the language of art's
evaluation, the means by which art is judged: in truth, memories are
never "judged"). Like the experience of an artwork, memory dissolves
the demands of the present. But, unlike the artwork, it effects this
dissolution by allowing a past moment to penetrate and be bound
to a present. Memory places the two separated moments together

but without disturbing their separation. Equally, as memory is indissociable from history (not the "flow of time," which it interrupts and arrests), memory itself is without such a history. One never recalls having had a particular memory in the past, even as one knows of moments that have often been remembered. A particular memory is always somehow new. The word "somehow," far from being gratuitous, is essential to the involuntary memory's mode of being present to the one who remembers.

The role of memory in the imagination of utopia (any utopia): memory's imprecision, its soft lines and curves, its gentle, diffused light. Adorno was correct in his linking of utopia to memories of childhood—when the child's life was without use and did not have use imposed upon it.

4.

T.K. leaves today. He is very nervous. Oddly, so am I. I have already begun to miss him. There is no time for words to be exploratory; now they are consolatory. I can see that he is facing in two directions: backward, on the adventure that has now all but concluded, and forward, to his arrival home. Between the past and the future: the Empty-time of waiting.

> «out of my dreams
> suns wandered,
> yet everything was gone
> when your day began.
> Everything remained unsaid.»
> ("Departure from England")

After the rainstorm: birdsongs and ambulance sirens.

I have managed to misplace a list I made earlier today at a café of subjects I want to write about in these pages. This annoys me. I can find the list nowhere. Earlier today I mislaid my cigarette lighter. After repeated searches in all the "usual" places, I found it in my shaving bag, to my surprise. Who knows where I might find my list of subjects. Until then, I will remain "listless" and "subjectless." These I can add to my other lessnesses.

S., when I fetched the keys to the flat: "Do you remember me? (in English). I: "Of course, I remember you" (in German). It seems that I will only remember her (in German), inasmuch as we have had no further contact for days.

"I wonder what sinister something is being cooked up in Carinthia."

As with T.K., good discussions often involve an invitation into someone's past, into, that is, an important memory. This form of contact, effected through words, intellect, and imagination, is thoroughly erotic.

Perhaps a movie tonight—if I'm in the mood for shoot-shoot, boom-boom, bang-bang-, kiss-kiss.

I've been gone just several days, and, in my absence, the three-and-a-half-year-old K. seems to have learned at least 100 words. On the telephone a short while ago, he exercised fully his new-found freedom of speech.

«The days will want to be longer.»
("March Stars")

5

«And so to what does your heart attest?
Between yesterday and tomorrow it swings,
soundless and strange,
and what it beats
is its fall out of time.» ("Fall Down, Heart")

In the Niedermayr store on Wiedenerhauptstrasse, where I'd gone yesterday to get a cord to charge my i-pod, I was waited upon by a kind of Wiener Prussian Wannabe who coolly ignored my questions and the answers I gave to his questions alike. Although I have experienced in Vienna this kind of frosty and aggressive indifference masked as professional expertise, its intimidating effect, despite its probable origins in resistance to class servitude, never ceases to make me nervous and angry. In the end, however, after much unpleasantness , I got the thing I needed in order that I might listen to the music that will enable me to forget occasions such as he presented. —A small victory, but a significant one.

(The little victories are those that count, we can tell ourselves without shame, for there are no "large victories" for us.)

7.30 pm: the sounds of cutlery on china plates behind open windows. That part of Vienna that is not watching football on wide-screen TV is eating its evening meal.
"Evening meal" (*Abendessen*) has a humble ring to it.

But, as everyone knows, for the person who is alone, eating a meal is little more than a chore to get through.

This word means: *the way some eyes cling to the light.*

«Harder days are coming.
The loan of mortgaged time
will come due on the horizon.»
("Mortgaged Time")

6.

This word means: *the sound of a dear voice that has suddenly arrived from long ago.*

This word means: *the fragrance certain looks leave on the surface of the skin.*

"Before we continue with today's lesson, we should take attendance."

When I woke at 6.30, I went to the window to examine the gathering clouds. Along Schleifmühlgaße, as it bends toward Margaretenstraße, all the buildings seemed to be convalescing. Thus, their striking, almost tactile, beauty.

Upon my arrival in this flat, I immediately mastered the complicated trick of lighting the burners on the stove. This morning, however, I failed repeatedly, using up almost an entire small box of matches, before I finally succeeded. Since then, I have failed twice again. Charred match sticks lay in a heap on the tile of the counter like a miniature pyre. I must come soon to a new accord with fire.

The early morning was so dark that I had to turn on the desk light. I sat there, drinking coffee, looking out the window in the unreserved beauty of time.

An identity not in crisis is an identity not worth having.

In my morning tranquillity the thought that sometimes I am able to live the freedom I imagined for myself so long ago.

I dreamt of K. playing on the stone floor of the attic where laundry was hanging. He was laughing and his laughter moved through the cross-hatching of shadows.

The young woman at the window of the flat across the Kuhnplatz: like me, in
her underwear. Our eyes met for a moment, then she disappeared.
Did she, as I had done, climb the stairs, put away the groceries, take
off her sweat-damp clothes, put on some music, and open the shades
and windows to allow into the flat the outside? For me, that "outside"
included her; for her, it included me.

"Hoodoo"—a word I should use more often.

How do I come to be wearing my father's ancient, scarred hands?

To the man in the audience who asked the question of all the readers: "When
did you call yourselves 'poets?', I should have answered, following
Marx: "In the very late night." To wit: In the morning, reader; in the
afternoon, teacher; in the evening, partner and father; in the night,
philosopher; in the very late night, poet.

"I don't call myself much of anything at all." (Daniel Day-Lewis
as Hawkeye Pierce/Natty Bumpo in *The Last of the
Mohicans.*)—Probably the best, because most truthful,
answer.

The elderly man in the out-of-fashion suit coat, tie, and plaid waistcoat, complete
with watch-fob, crossing Rechte Wienzeile in the humid morning
with such a lordly grace. I could not but ask myself what he had to be
so proud of. Is age, by itself, something of which to be proud? I don't
think so. Moreover, his was such a humourless visage that I couldn't
even imagine a desire to talk to him about what was, perhaps, a life
richly lived.

In the paper shop where I went to get a good-quality paper for writing letters,
the woman was so kind that I felt I should purchase all of the many
papers she had, with such pride, brought out and displayed for me.

18

This word means: *the sound of her reflection separating from the shop window.*

I ran into B. on Margaretenstraße. That, in itself, was quite exceptional, but that
        we stood on the corner talking desultorily for almost an hour about
        all manner of things—H.'s health, B.'s new work, my new poems, the
        history of the Freihaus Viertel, music at the Schönberg Haus, Joseph
        Roth's last writings, Mahler's off-hours in the Café Sperl, Stifter's
        clouds, Ingeborg Bachmann's poems, etc.—well, is there a word for
        that, I wonder.

"Random acts of communication:" writing postcards from my Nowhere and
        Nowhen.

Although she is "striking" and gives every impression of wanting to be such, she
        is neither "beautiful" nor "well-preserved" (a truly macabre term).
        Rather the impression I have of her attempt to be so *visible* is that she is
        well-staffed: a product of the people and the products at her service.

He told himself that he really should try to smoke less and drink less. Then
        he told himself that in Vienna to do either seemed impossible.
        Perhaps, he said to himself, he might just as well try to see less, hear
        less, feel less, think less: to make of himself, through subtraction, an
        "accomplishment."

This word means: *the tones of raindrops rattling in the wind.*

I would rather listen to the sounds of children at play in the Platz beneath my
        window than to the sounds of the Fußbol fans moaning and cheering
        in the Café Anzengruber across the street. Perhaps I should plug one
        ear—the older one!

The broad smile filling his face as we approached each other: how could I ever
        forget that?

The separation of beauty from morality (moral goodness) has been healthily ignored only by poets, saints, and madmen—much to the shame of modern philosophy and its practitioners.

Moments of true happiness: ambling and standing still under no one's honest white clouds.

As they sit down, each removes a cell-phone (he from the inside pocket of his tailored sports coat, she from her designer leather handbag) and places it on the table. Thus do they state wordlessly to each other their importance and authority. Now they are ready to talk "seriously."

After my long walk in the opposite direction, I was too tired to refresh myself on the terrace of the Café Sperl. —One of today's regrets.

No one is supposed to see other than his coiffed silver hair, his tailored sand-coloured silk suit, his oversized, chunky stainless-steel watch, the gold ring on his little finger, and the Italian leather shoes on his feet; in other words, no one is to see other than the signs of wealth and power and his own ease with them. On the other hand, if one has the proper squint, he is really little more than a collection of accessories. He does not want to be *seen*; he wants to be *imagined*—but only according to the instructions his *accoutrements* transmit.

The clouds reflected in the windows of the flats on the upper storeys of the building on the other side of Kühnplatz: bubbling orange and a floating fire of roses. Turbulent descendants of Stifter's tranquil floating worlds.

At around 9.00 p.m., she took her sunglasses from their perch in her hair, scratched her head, and returned them to the self-same spot from which she had removed them. When I asked why she put them on her head again, considering that the sun had set some time ago, she answered, "But these are Armani."

Postcards should be made of the displays in the windows of the Palmers'
stores. They would say much about Vienna's consciousness—and its
unconscious.

In Vienna, the "naughty" and the "lofty" embrace again and again. Well, that's all
I know.

Her shadow scratched its head—I saw it—as she listened to the man across the
table from her. Then it rose and walked away.

«A handful of pain disappears over the hill.»
("Early Noon")

7

Sometimes, for no real reason, a kind of low-level panic. Then I must work up courage just to leave the flat. Once I'm in the street, even if I have nowhere in particular to go, calm returns. I can get ahead of my anxiety.

"Meet us by the statue of the saint holding down a large serpent with one foot. There is an ice cream parlour just to one side of it."

As T.K. and I were talking, the sudden roar of fighter jets passing just over the rooftops, growing deafeningly loud. He looked me straight in the eye. "This is death," he shouted. And for a moment that was empty of fear—surprisingly—I thought he was right.

In one of her poems, Bachmann wrote of death being "sealed" in a "fanfare of noise."

The sporadic banging of open windows being closed by the wind. I keep expecting to hear a crash, followed by the tinkling of broken glass.

In one hour and a half, I will have been here for a week, but it seems only a few hours have passed since I arrived, as if time has folded in on itself.

Now I can almost identify all the ring-tones of the telephones in the surrounding apartments. I can hear them when the windows are open.

I thought I heard pigeons cooing loudly on a nearby window ledge, but a sudden bellow told me I was wrong. The sound I heard was that of my downstairs neighbour reaching orgasm.

Think of it this way: today, in the street, I can be sheltered by those ominous-
looking clouds wherever I go.

Buildings with eyebrows. Curving streets. Short streets. Lanes. Small gardened
squares in unexpected places. A young woman reading a book on one
of the benches there in the shade of a plane tree. The sight of her so
pleasant that I want to stop and chat a while, just to be a participant in
such tranquillity.

The cigarette package says, "*Toujours Liberté.*" The beer bottle says, "*Ein Glass
heller Freude.*" My vices tell me that I've come to the right place. (But:
would a true vice say otherwise?)

A day so mean with light.

The woman sitting with her friends at the table next to mine has perceived that I
am a stranger. She asks where I come from. I tell her. She compliments
my German. I thank her, adding that my German is a bit rusty. She asks
if I am here "for the *Fußbol.*" I say that I am not. "So why did you come
to Vienna?" she asks. "To read," I answer. She laughs a good one and
turns to her friends, saying "This man has come all the way to Vienna
from Canada just to read! He must be crazy, I think." Her friends look
at me quizzically. All I can do is shrug my shoulders. I cannot, after all,
disagree with her blunt assessment. But because this chance encounter
is amusing, she is not yet finished with me. "So, what do you read?" she
asks. I will be truthful, I decide. I mention Bachmann, Handke, and
several other Austrian writers. She nods. "Yes, now I understand," she
says. "They are crazy, too."

Moments of small pleasure: to see from the height of the window how the
shadows of the people walking in the street below catch up to them,
meld with them for the distance of a few paces, then outdistance them.

K: "Catch my shadow, Daddy."

I have become a student of shadows and echoes.

As I awoke from the nap I had drifted into, I was startled by the thought that no one was here to be afraid with me.

This word means: *the light left in the other room.*

This word means: *the warmth left in the door handle by the hand that just touched it.*

I awoke feeling as if I'd failed in my purpose: to retrieve sleep from the cold place into which it had vanished.

Now it is the hour of shadows mingling with each other.

"As if a tender nudge could awaken the night...."

This word means: *the smile lingering in the air from the person who just greeted you.*

As I spoke with A., I rested my hand on the handlebars of her bicycle. Then my action struck me as a violation of etiquette. I feared it might be taken as an effrontery, yet I was even more afraid to withdraw it hastily for fear that might make more conspicuous its unintended transgression. In my dilemma, I absent-mindedly raised my hand to my head and ran it through my hair. All my anxiety disappeared, and I was able again to be happy to see her.

This word means: *you've been too long in the flat alone, and now you must go outside for a while.*

K. told me that he wants to go to "Picnic Island" with mommy and me "because no grown-ups live on Picnic Island."

She sits down at a corner table as daylight weakens. She is "sedate" and "composed" (really the only adequate description). The glass of white wine she ordered arrives. She thanks the server with her eyes only. She is waiting, sipping the wine occasionally. Soon the waiting will end: at the appointed hour, as they always do, Reverie and Memory will arrive to charm her.

Today has been a Malone-ish day. (The End.)

>>The uniform of the day is patience,
the order of merit is the wretched star
of hope over the heart.

It is awarded
when nothing more happens.<<
("Every Day")

8.

In my dream I was walking on the same little back street along which I had
walked days ago. In the dream, the street was as empty as it had been in
reality. But when I suddenly emerged into Margaretenstraße, so much
noise and so many people confused me that I turned in the wrong
direction. I knew it was the "wrong" direction, but I persisted despite
this knowledge. Soon I was no longer anxious about being lost, and
a voice said, "There's no need to worry. You are a diligent student of
wrong directions."

A small smear of time.

I could have sworn that the hands on the clock had stopped, fallen backward,
stopped again, gone ahead, stopped again, fallen back again, stopped
once more, gone ahead again ....

To have a conversation with someone as if your whole life depended upon it.

K: "Put your hand on my head, Daddy. Can you feel me growing?"

We were abreast of each other because the flow of pedestrian traffic in the
Naschmarkt had come to a stop in both directions. I smiled at her
and laughed. She, too, laughed and said, "This one is for you" as she
put a strawberry in my mouth. The traffic started to move again, and
we went, laughing, in our separated directions, a sweet and luscious
moment in our mouths.

As I stood behind the stout older woman who was also buying cheese, I saw the
flakes of whitewash on her elbows. She, too, had been leaning on her
windowsill this morning.

This word means: *the dreams of an empty bed.*

«since we endure an order that cannot heal or teach»
("Night Flight")

Like many European cities that were partially destroyed during World War Two,
Vienna responded by making "exact replicas" of buildings that were
blown to smithereens. (The Opera House and the Albertina are the
best-known examples.) But restoration of the glories of the Past (even
if the building is put to different uses, such as the Albertina) is not
the only evidence in Vienna of the ubiquity of history. Here, the old
and the new are not only juxtaposed or contiguous; it is often the case
that the latter inhabit, literally, the structure of the former. This is not
only a matter of, for example, the "renovation" of private apartments
in buildings that may be more than 150 or 200 years old; it is also the
case of buildings that serve a more "public" function. Here the old and
the new dance a waltz all their own. A shop specializing in women's
sexy underwear occupies the ground floor of a neo-Baroque building
that once housed a bank; a private, high-brow photography gallery is
located in an eighteenth century building complete with columns and
caryatids; a building Beethoven could have passed on his numerous
forays through the streets of the city contains a photocopying service.
Many other examples could be given. According to a pragmatic and
positivist view, these examples merely prove history's continuity,
its going-on through (necessary) alteration, its answering to new
demands. But from another viewpoint, not the continuity but the
anachronism is the striking feature one feels when looking about this
city. The old and the new dance here cheek-to-cheek, but each partner
whispers into the other's ear words of an unknown, unknowable,
language. The rest is laughter.

Here I must ask: With whom, with what, am I "contemporary?"

This word means: *the ache of the knife.*

I have swept all the rooms of the flat, washed by hand underwear, socks, and
a shirt, drunk coffee, gone to the market, returned, put away the
provisions—and my two loves are still asleep in our home so far away.

«Call it the status of the lonely
in whom wonder still occurs.
Nothing more.»
("Night Flight")

As I crossed Linke Wienzeile on my way to the market, the two guys drinking
beer at a small table in front of the Grafin am Naschmarkt turned
toward me, sized me up, and, having decided I was no threat, returned
to their breakfast. It was 9.30 a.m., and I had the feeling that I'd already
survived the worst the day might offer.

Overheard in the Naschmarkt this morning: a young woman speaking to an
older woman (perhaps her mother): "I've come all this way, and no
one will speak German to me." Older woman: "They're only being
kind." Young woman: "No, that's not it. They just want my money."
Older woman: "Well, English is the language of money, dear."

The orange juice is named "Happy Day." The bread is named "Harry."

A memory of K. taking pebbles from his pocket. He gives one to me, saying,
"My find a crystal for you, daddy."

Money, keys to the building, keys to the flat, sweater (in case of sudden cold),
umbrella (in case of sudden rain), guidebook, dictionary, city map,
notebooks (the small one for taking into the galleries), pen, cigarettes,
lighter, book (Celan's translations of Mandelshtam)—all these *items* to
complete me before I even open the door.

Cops talking on cell phones.

It would not surprise me to learn that all these people who wear large designer
sunglasses never remove them, not even when they make love—so
much do they seem like features of their faces. (Well, perhaps to make
love, they would "bed" their sunglasses in their hair.)

(Come to think of it, wearing sunglasses during sex might be a
widespread fantasy.)

«. . . not the immortals,
but rather the fallen we perceive.»
("Message")

History makes victims and silences them: with that recognition, which you
will not forget, you can look again at the castles, the museums, the art
galleries, the statues and the monuments, etc.

I don't understand how any Christian, i.e., anyone who viewed the painting
when he made it, could not have been perfectly and completely
terrified by Bosch's *Last Judgement*. Who today would—could—make
a picture (or any other work of art) with such a terrifying effect? Who
would dare to? (Hermann Nitsch, et. al. seem mere children when
compared to Bosch.) The sheer number and variety of the tortures
carried out by the demons—the slicings, skewerings, piercings,
twistings, bindings, roastings, boilings, cagings, and more—originate
in the everyday actions of those on whom they are, on the Day
of Reckoning, being performed. The "order" of their world has
been turned against them, and they are truly abandoned. Every act
necessary to survival has become, when survival has already been
cancelled, purely murderous.

Is it safe to say that Bosch's horrors are even more vivid after the
decline of Christianity? The early viewers of the painting could repent
their sinful ways and choose the "correct path," after all. But when faith
in the "correct path" no longer exists, what remains? A nightmare of
cruelty and suffering without end? —Or just "Art?"

No one is more talented at revealing a person's pseudo-spontaneity than a young
child.

A dove has just alighted on the window box. I think to myself: Now I know I will
dream again.

A woman on the café terrace yawns. Soon everyone but the servers are also
yawning. One by one, the customers fall quietly asleep at their tables.
The servers sit down to chat among themselves and smoke. Some
drink coffee; others, lemonade. They keep their voices low and hushed
so as not to awaken the sleepers. In the same order in which they fell
to sleep, the people at the tables raise their heads and open their eyes.
The servers are on their feet, circulating among the tables, removing
cups, glasses, plates, bringing new orders of food and drink. Bills
are requested, presented, and paid. The customers depart as new
customers arrive. Dream-time is ended.

> «Wherever we turn in the storm of roses,
> the night is lighted by thorns, and the thunder
> of leaves, once so quiet in the bushes,
> now follows at our heels.»
> ("In the Storm of Roses")

All the beggars are not old, but they are all maimed, making their crippled ways
from table to table, hands outstretched, palms up, where they are
pointedly ignored.

The sight of even a single beggar provides deeper insights into history than those
obtained in years of lecture halls and seminar rooms.

9.

This word means: *the sound of a misty rain falling on the empty streets at 5.00 a.m.*
       this Sunday morning.

     Q: So why did you come to Vienna?
     A: To hear the ringing of the all the church bells on Sunday morning.

     Q: So why did you come to Vienna?
     A: To be alone here, alone and anonymous.

     Q: So why did you come to Vienna?
     A: To listen in a different language.

     Q: So why did you come to Vienna?
     A: To be absent but not dead.
     Q: Ah, now I understand.

Mother to Child: "Please pick up all the words you left lying on the floor."

Slowly, the street is waking. And here comes a woman wearing a short, tight skirt
       and knee-high boots, marching right through it all. Now everything
       can truly appear.

Ing. came by last evening to see how I was doing in the flat. My telephone
       card didn't work for her either, and we both concluded that I'd been
       swindled. She will help me by trying to get the money (40 euros)
       back. She noticed the book of Celan translations of Mandelshtam
       and a volume of Ingeborg Bachmann's poems on the table. A good
       conversation ensued. But when the word "vulnerable" was uttered, we
       both knew that it had reached its end, and we could say no more.

If ever I really knew how to relax, that knowledge, too, has deserted me.

The pattern of the Turkish carpets on the floor: continents floating on a sea of
  wood.

When she sat down at the table in the café's terrace, she leaned back in the chair,
  slipped off her shoes, and wiggled her toes—a gesture that restored
  her girlhood to her. When the server came to take her order, she sat up
  straight and slipped her feet back into her shoes. When the server had
  left, she slipped off only one shoe.

  Q: So why did you come to Vienna?
  A: To prepare for my aging and death.
  Q: Can one really prepare for one's death?
  A: I can't honestly answer that question. But if one can prepare for
    death, Vienna seems a good place to pick up some pointers.

Contented for a time just to sit at this table, sip this cool white wine, look out the
  open window, and breathe.

This word means: *the chill you suddenly felt when you turned onto the shady side
  street.*

The squeaks of the floorboards underfoot: each has a different pitch.

Disappointed not to know the name of this bird so generous with song.

  Q: So why did you come to Vienna?
  A: To be perplexed—but in a manner different from my normal
    perplexity.

The child fell down and suffered a small hurt on her knee. Now she berates her
  mother in high volume for having "allowed" it to happen.

I stopped talking to myself and began talking to the bird that was singing so
      beautifully and haltingly among the flowers.

They were standing on the sidewalk as if facing each other, but their faces were
      turned away. They said nothing. To guess what they might be feeling
      at that moment was difficult, for their eyes were hidden behind
      sunglasses. After a long moment, he reached across the gulf between
      them and took her hand. As people passed them by in both directions,
      he kissed each of her fingertips. She laughed and put her arm
      around his neck. On they walked, each in the embrace of the other's
      forgiveness. —All the religion anyone could ever need.

      Q: So why did you come to Vienna?
      A: To find a place where I could get lost and feel less real.

Yes, those people are really wearing jackets and scarves in Vienna on Sunday, 15.
      June 2008.

In the Karlskirche: it is difficult to know if those in attendance are here out of
      a sense of devotion or out of a love for music. As for me, the music
      works far better than the service from which I separate it with a
      lowering of my eyelids.

The old man beside me is breathing to the cellos.

Outside the church after the service, the woman whose breasts I took notice of
      is fondling the ass of a man who is talking to another woman standing
      next to a man talking on his cell phone. All of them break into laughter
      seconds apart from each other with different people about different
      things.

But: so many here who seem to be at home in their suffering.

The Church: a locus not just of sin and suffering but also of sex and money.

Upon leaving the church: everyone sets fire to a cigarette and sets off for
  something to eat and drink.

This word means: *the patience of the wine glass as it awaits her lips.*

«I see borderless music
in the movement of the mute.»
("A Monologue of Prince Myshkin to the Ballet Pantomime
'The Idiot'")

The truck is named "Friedl."

The feeling of relief (or release?) upon walking out of a church even now, at my
  age: incomparable. It stirs up memories from childhood: "Now we can
  play!"

Last night, for the third night in a row, he did not turn on a light, he did not
  light a candle, he did not read; he sat in the dark room like a piece
  of its furniture. He sat as if in the prolonged stillness of death. And
  he remembered—each thing, each touch, each word, each sound,
  each smell, each taste—; he remembered everything as it would be
  remembered by the dead.

"Please, I am from Linz," he told me as he approached me early in the morning
  on Kühnplatz. His black suitcoat was at least two sizes too small, and
  the bottom of his trousers was not even in shouting distance of his
  ankles. "I came here to find some friends, but they are gone. I cannot
  find them." His hands fluttering like white birds to his face, his hair;
  his eyes looking at me then looking away; at me, away. "Please," he
  continued, "I need to get back … my mother … my sister…. Please, a
  train …. Can you help me?" I take from my pocket all the coins I have,
  about eight euros. He holds the coins in his hand. "Please, these are
  not heavy enough."

Just for a brief time earlier today such a sense of aloneness and dread that I was
paralysed, and I understood why T., alone in Paris, lost control of
himself, suffered a complete mental and emotional collapse, and had to
be flown home by the authorities. That thought (somehow) restored
me to myself, and all my anxiety evaporated.

In the restaurant where B. and I ate dinner, the very formal waiter, on seeing my
empty plate, asked in English, "Are you finished?" I replied without
thinking, "*Nein, aber ich bin ein bischen müde.*" ("No, but I'm a bit
tired."). He looked at me uncomprehendingly, then took away my
plate. "Well," said B., laughing. "I don't think he was expecting that."

In one of his finer (or madder) moments, my father would have drawn my
attention to the similarity to each other of all the Christs on all the
Crosses in the churches of Europe and North America, emphasizing
the Messiah's barely-covered loins, the absence of body hair, the long,
almost effeminate, smooth white torso, the nails in the suffering hands
and feet, the open spear-wound in his side, the blood on his shoulders
and chest, face and neck, flowing from his head with its crown of
thorns, the expression of agony in the exhausted face, the utter
forsakenness in the upturned gaze. All of this evidence would lead him
to the conjecture that one company was responsible for reproducing
from moulds, in different sizes, the dying body of our lord, and for
painting its crimson blood, its brown hair, and its blue eyes, and this
company was owned by the Catholic Church which, in any case,
was nothing more than a factory mass-producing not only plaster
dying gods but also sin, guilt, and misery, all of which is certainly evil
in itself, but insult is added to injury by the millions upon millions
of dollars it squeezes from those it makes suffer. —Then he would
probably have poured himself another stiff whiskey. Into the glass, as
he raised it to his lips, he would have muttered, "How goddam right
does one little human have to be?"

Sunday: Bachmann wrote once that it was "every lost day" ("Of a Land, a
River, and Lakes"). Certainly that "lostness" contains something of
an effrontery to the biblical "day of rest." Sunday morning strikes one
with the emptiness of streets, their pervasive silence, their abundant
absences. It might once have been a day of "interiority," of delving

one's own "soul" to its bottoms through communication with whatever Almighty in which one happened to believe. It may once have been a day one spent in solitude with oneself and with one's family. But self and family are no less *absconditus* than the very deity whose "rest" after the hard work of creation this day was meant to honour. "Sunday" names the designation of every empty time one has ever endured. Sunday's quietude is the storehouse of every stranded moment: it is on Sunday, in its emptiness and its silence, that the chafing against each other of all such moments cannot be mistaken.

To come away from a conversation and realize as I am walking down the street that I have just had a very special gift bestowed upon me.

Q: So why did you come to Vienna?
A: To know the shadows absence casts.
Q: To cast such a shadow yourself?
A: Perhaps.
Q: Vienna eats shadows. It thrives on them.

«Everyone who falls has wings.»
("The Game is Over")

10.

7.15 a.m. and the shadow of a bird flying past the window just crossed this page.

The traffic sounds in the street below mean it's a workday. Soon the garbage trucks will pass.

The young man walks quickly down the street, one hand pulling a bundle-buggy containing his purchases from the market, the other hand pulling a leash attached to which is a very small brown dog.

Today I noticed for the first time that the shop of the grouchy candy dealer is gone and that the mailboxes in the foyer are shiny and new. Then I began to wonder what else I had not noticed.

When I gathered all the postcards I've accumulated since I arrived, the stack made me think of the two bumpkins in Godard's film (*Les carabiniers*?) who return home from the wars with their "booty:" a suitcase full of postcard reproductions of art "treasures."

Benjamin's statement, "There is no document of civilization that is not at the same time a document of barbarism," should, perhaps, be affixed over the front of the door of every museum (not only art museums) in the world as a reminder to all those who enter it that it is a monument built over an abyss.

When I looked out the window, I was happy to see that all the shops, restaurants, and people were in their proper places.

"You be wightning and my be dunder, okay, daddy?"

"I take a line and go for a walk with it" (Paul Klee).

The long duration and intensity of the child's crying and screaming––that
mixture of ferocity and abjection. I thought immediately of K. Then I
thought of the child's parents' despair.

From its location on the tabletop, his hand contemplates her face.

B., talking to me of the eroticism of the works of Schiele and Klimt, used the
word "unashamed." He spoke it as a throw-away word, but I was struck
with the full force of its truth.

As she passed me in the street, I overheard the old woman say to herself, "The
light was very feeble today."

The crowd of people standing and milling about on the sidewalk in front of the
café, each talking on a cell-phone: this is a truly curious little drama (or
perhaps ballet). Configurations form and dissolve. Some people stand
firmly in place; others wander a distance away; still others, walking,
almost collide with people likewise absorbed in conversation with
an absence. The absent-minded gestures—the head-scratching, the
fingernail inspection, the scanning of faces, the looking away from
faces, the making of little adjustments to clothing—are on display.
Everyone is speaking, listening, and gesturing, but none to his/her
neighbour. Dumb-show with cell-phones.

In the dusk, an old man with curly grey hair, wearing a suit coat and a scarf,
comes riding a child's scooter very *carefully* along the sidewalk, a wide
grin spread across his face.

A light that does not destroy the dark but illuminates it.

11.

A sudden memory of K. asking me, "Daddy, where is the end of far?

This word means: *a tangle of cloud and light.*

In the Karlskirche on Sunday, I was present only to listen to the music and the
  singing. As for the Mass itself, I was only an eavesdropper in much the
  same way as one unintentionally overhears people talking in a café, on
  a bus, or in a subway car. But I would very much like to have been one
  of Wender's angels, listening in to the thoughts of the church-goers,
  many of which, I am certain, had little or nothing to do with heaven,
  sin, god, or saintliness.

Jean-Luc Godard's "To look around one is to live free" could be the motto of
  any tourist or visitor to a foreign place, if only because such a person
  is already "free" to look around. His statement assumes a salutary
  form and degree of alienation. To this notion of freedom could easily
  be added the practice of "listening around." Freedom is the giving of
  attention without compulsion or fear.

With one hand, she raised her coffee cup to her lips; with the other, she gripped
  the edge of the table as if the winds of an approaching storm that only
  she could see would carry her away.

That I appear to have lost 35 euros today is the direct result of:
  A: never knowing how much cash I have in my possession at any given
      time;
  B: always knowing how much cash I have in my possession at any
      given time;
  C: spending my cash impulsively;
  D: all of the above

For a time this morning, around 11.00, the light was generous; no other word can describe it.

T.K. referred to himself as a "Hatha-Yodeler."

"Alone all day with your hands:" I wrote that line in a poem twenty-four years ago. Only now do I think I know what I meant.

This word means: *the lingering of the music in the air long after the playing of it has stopped.*

When I inquired of the clerk in the paper shop about blank notebooks I might bring home as gifts, he proudly showed me his display of notebooks from Canada. The notebooks were fair copies of an increasingly popular high-quality European notebook, but the paper was of inferior quality. When I told him that my home was in Canada but that I'd never seen such notebooks there, I saw suspicion sweep into his eyes: he did not believe me; he did not want to believe me. I thought for a moment that he was going to demand to see my passport.

The breeze on the terrace is gentle, the leaves rustle overhead, people pass, my thoughts are not too restless, so I will have another *Viertel* of this delicious white wine—a privilege of one who is separated from obligation. I can drift in this moment as earlier I drifted through history's streets.

The exhibition of more than 150 of Paul Klee's drawings at the Albertina has made me wonder: can such a thing as *profound amusement* exist? If it can, it is to be encountered through these works.

The large group of elderly people in the museum today: they do not so much look at a work, study it, or examine it: they *swarm* it, all gathering before it and exchanging comments about it (some of which have to be repeated at a higher volume because some of the members of the swarm are hard of hearing). These old folks behave like teenagers— but without the smirks, giggles, and sudden explosions of laughter.

The older man standing before the El Lissitsky, shaking his head from side to side: a judgement of the painting? Later, I recognize him in front of a Monet: he is smiling. I couldn't help but do the same when I saw his happiness at the rendering of such beauty. Despite all that separates us (age, language, culture, history), we can inhabit the same self-less moment, the one beauty opened to us.

With Klee, amusement (or is it enchantment?) deepens in at least three ways. First, the longer one looks, the more one sees of the lines and figures and the more of the relationships among them one is able to grasp. This is true of all art, but it does not deprive Klee's works of their eccentricity and idiosyncrasy. Even as one is able to see more, one gets the feeling that much remains elusive or invisible. Abstract lines, curves, etc. conjure a concrete object while remaining abstract. The viewer of Klee's work cannot occupy the space of a master. Secondly, the titles of the works often reinforce this elusive quality. One has the sense that the drawings themselves are, somehow, in motion: even as they "come" to you, you feel they are already departing, perhaps even fleeing. Thirdly, the more one is able to see, the higher one's spirits and thoughts are raised, so that the original feeling of amusement is not at all displaced by the state of intellectual joy to which it has, through a number of curious manoeuvres, led. In some cases, the odd but nevertheless strong feeling that a drawing had seen and "oogled" the viewer as he/she entered the room, not suspecting that a certain adventure was in store and he/she was about to be caught off guard, is difficult to shake off.

Before my eyes—no, *in* my eyes—the old woman looking out her open window in the apartment across the Platz was suddenly transformed into the beautiful young girl she once was. —And so she remains, and will always remain.

41

If the number of pages I could write in a day equalled the number of cigarettes I can smoke, I would remain in the blooming of contentment.

A relief: not to see anyone wearing a baseball cap, not to mention anyone wearing a baseball cap backwards.

With his close-cropped thick white hair, slight stoop and shuffling walk, and a face creased and crossed with wrinkles, he is the figure of an elderly man in polished old brown shoes and a well-worn blue pinstriped, double-breasted suit a bit too large for him. But his eyes say otherwise. Lively and grey, they say that he has not, as do many elderly persons, retreated to a place somewhere far behind their eyes. His eyes say that he is fully present, wherever he happens to be.

On this bright, warm day, he has just entered the Café Mozart where no one has taken notice of his slow walk to the room's centre, where he now stands, those grey eyes surveying the busy, noisy room. From table to table, where couples and groups, young, middle-aged, and old are eating, drinking, talking, laughing, and smoking, his eyes move. He stands stock-still, only his eyes moving from table to table, from face to face.

His voice, when he starts to speak, is also still and quiet, as soft as if he were seated at a table and conversing with a friend. His hands at his sides, he begins to tell the story of this café to those gathered within it. He says that this café is the scene of a crime. He tells how the Café Mozart, once called the Café Sans Souci, was built and owned by a Jew. He tells that after the annexation in 1938, the café was "Aryanized," and its name was changed to the name it still bears today. He tells that the new ownership of the hotel was registered in the name of a Nazi semi-illiterate chimney-sweep. He tells that the original owner of the café was murdered in a concentration camp.

As he tells this story, only his eyes and mouth move. Slowly, the people at the tables become quiet. They put down their forks and knives and glasses to listen to the words coming from this bent old man. When he has finished, only uneasy silence. A silence that is not merely the absence of noise and words. The old man has spoken to them the silence that has been housed in this café, in every inch of its floors, its walls, its tables, its mirrors. He has spoken the undestroyed silence.

The eyes of some stare at the old man, the eyes of others are averted, downward to tables or outward through the windows to the passers-by. No one looks at another's face; no one looks in another's eyes.

The spell of the thickening silence is broken by the sound of a throat being cleared. Soon after, the sounds of cutlery scraping plates, whispered words, the tinkling of glasses, and small bursts of laughter emerge. The words and the noise grow louder. The eating, drinking, talking, and smoking have resumed; all the normal activities of a café's cosy relations are restored to it. Here and there, raucousness erupts.

The old man has vanished, as if into thin air.

As if every smile, laugh, bite of food, and sip from cup or glass utters an oath that he was never there, never there at all.

This word means: *that part of her shadow nestling into the wall that received it as she passed.*

12.

The sun is late for our morning rendezvous.

The echoing in the halls of the apartment doors being closed and locked: a
    sound I recognize as belonging also to cheap hotels.

So tired last night but unable to fall asleep. The post-football match revellers
    singing and shouting along the street; laughter and breaking glass. I lay
    awake, day-dreaming that I was sleeping and dreaming.

I watched for a long time a spider making its web in a corner of the room
    beneath the window. I watched for so long, in fact, that I forgot I was
    watching. When I realized this, I had the thoroughly silly feeling that
    I'd done the spider an injustice.

Before the shops, before the stalls in the Naschmarkt, before the restaurants
    and most of the cafés, before the banks and the Post Office, before the
    churches—I was "open."

The woman who works in the bakery where I went for croissants—for a
    moment she seemed to caress the bread.

The young man in the park gave me what I took to be a defiant "Fuck you" look
    when he saw that I saw he had no plastic bag to clean up his dog's shit.
    I had caught him out by looking when I was not supposed to look and
    by seeing what I was not supposed to see.

Alone at the table in the mid-morning, not fully here, not anywhere else—I am
    where I can be: immersed in matter's music.

Mature men, grey-haired and white-haired, in expensive suits, riding their
bicycles with graceful ease.

The somewhat depressing thought that for many of the people who have come
here from elsewhere a pleasant memory they will take home with
them is that of sipping a take-out coffee from Starbuck's as they stroll
past the shop windows on Kärtnerstraße and Mariahilferstraße.

Where is the Museum of Failures, Errors, Botches, Confusions, and Mistakes?
A Museum of Lost Moments , Despairs, and Perished Possibilities,
would be, I think, a welcome corrective to our "civilization."

The gaps between the sound of a motorcycle starting and a truck accelerating are
filled by this bird's full-throated singing.

This word means: *the sound of footsteps slowing and turning a corner in the dark of
night.*

Walking away, she shouted back to him, "I'm tired of you trying to *Something*
me."

Another relief: to be in a place where people do not carry bottles of water and
sip from them repeatedly.

The little girl walking down the street with her hand in her father's hand
suddenly stopped, gave her schoolbag to her father, and pulled down
her pants to adjust her underwear. As I approached, he looked from
her to me, his smile made of equal parts protectiveness, exasperation,
and embarrassment.

The tiny beads of perspiration on the bare shoulders and back of the violinist.

A word in the dark, filled with footsteps.

The two women police officers, one in heavy black boots, the other in shoes that resemble ballet slippers.

This word means: *The storm of the many shades of green in the tree beneath which, on a bench, the young lovers are sitting.*

If anyone should ever ask, I can say that once, at least, I know I was imagined.

The model of the Citroën van that almost hit me this morning as it came out of a lane onto Wiedner Hauptstraße bore the name "Picasso." Had it been called "Dürer", that "close call" might not have happened. Then again, had it been called "Kandinsky" or "Miró," I might no longer exist.

Whenever I hear Beethoven's Ninth Symphony, I also hear the jubilant ovation it ignited at its premiere in 1824, one that has lasted to this very day.

If S. were here with me, I would probably have tarried longer in the antiques store. Only after I'd trudged home did I realize that I'd missed the opportunity to be found by a displaced treasure.

Aware that I am more than a little bit lost on a street strange to me, I think I will ask directions at the mechanic's garage just a short distance ahead. But when I get closer to the two men there, I can see that this is a moment I should not interrupt. The older man (the boss) is explaining to the younger man (the employee) that he is "much disappointed" in the younger man's work. As I pass them by, the younger man looks at me and shrugs his shoulders, as if to say, "There he goes, acting like a boss again. For some people there is no salvation." —A wisdom he has learned early.

Those are very tight jeans this young woman is wearing, and, though they
definitely fit her well, I cannot help but wonder at the amount of
effort and time expended to get them on and to get them off. Do their
seams leave imprints on her calves, thighs, and hips? Do the shapes
stitched on the rear leave impressions on her buttocks when she
sits?—I hear myself asking these questions—incredibly—in the voice
of my mother! My mother, who spoke nostalgically of the dances she
attended as a young woman where "girdles could be checked" with
the coats and hats. She would say this with a giggle and laugh out loud
at the memory of it, hearing again in her mind the music of Tommy
Dorsey, Jimmy Dorsey, Benny Goodman—the music to which her
favourite memories, as her eyes told me, danced.

On a busy sidewalk, a man pushes a doorbell on a panel beside the door. When,
after a few minutes, he hears no signal to open the door, he takes out
his cell-phone and pushes some buttons. Shortly, a man talking on a
cell-phone opens a window on the third floor. The two men talk to
each other on their cell-phones, one man looking up, the other man
looking down. After five minutes or so, the man on the street places
his cell-phone in a pocket and walks away. The other man closes the
window.

This word means: *the weight the leaf exerts on the air after it has broken from the
tree.*

I could not but think that everything about the elderly bookseller was kindly—
not only her voice, her hands, her face and eyes, but even her slight
stoop, for it renders the look she gives to be one of curiosity, alertness,
and genuine interest. To be met with such a look is a rarity.

The silence left behind in the empty tram car.

In the Kleines Café I keep my promise to H. I lift my glass, and, inwardly, I make
a toast to her, looking her in the eye the whole while.

This word means: *the music she hears when a pleasant memory suddenly overtakes her.*

"... the utopia of not being oneself." (Adorno)

In all the photos I have ever seen of him, I am always surprised to see a gentleness in Thomas Bernhardt's face.

"I never really liked her...." "And when I woke up, he was on top of me...." "Darling, let me talk to daddy, please...." "I am here for almost an hour. Where are you?..." "I had better check my messages...." "No, to Italy...." "She kicked him out of the flat, she really did...." "This thing is not working...." "No, no. They are waiting. I have to go...." —Human voices rising through my night.

Walking down a quiet, tree-lined street, a man and a woman are having the kind of disagreement composed of a great deal of accusatory silence, which each of them resents. Inevitably, they arrive at a corner of the street, where they stop. Neither moves in any direction. They look at each other and look away. The woman takes a cell-phone from her shoulder bag and presses a button. The cell-phone in the man's jacket pocket beeps. He takes out the cell-phone and answers her call. They face each other, each speaking into his/her cell-phone. Then she turns her back, still talking. He turns in the opposite direction, also talking. Simultaneously, they begin to walk away from each other, still talking, until they are both out of sight to each other and to everyone.

This word means: *the sleep of a shadow.*

48

13.

At this hour (7.00) yesterday morning, all was so very quiet. But today
    everything and everyone is up and out and making noise. Even the
    sunlight seems noisy.

He tells himself that he must find a way to slow down his feelings.

> «We were light as birds, heavy as trees,
> as bold as dolphins and as still as eggs,
> We were dead but living, now a being
> And now a thing. (We will never be free!).»
> ("Of a Land, a River and Lakes")

Bach's Violin Partitas dancing through the traffic sounds contaminates them
    with grace.

At 8.30 in the morning, two attractive young women in sleek and slinky dresses
    are sauntering and laughing along the street, where no one even gives
    them a second look.

Two friends are just sitting down to their 9.00 a.m. beer.

My "self-experiment."

The recurring fantasy that everyone—literally—is employed by the Vienna
    Tourist Bureau to promote the city just by doing what they do and by
    being who they are.

Thought and reverie: fraternal twins.

The tedium of the merriment of the *Fußbol* fans—there, I've said it.

Strange undertow to the conversation with A. last night—as if we were both
trying to break out of the false identity that we sensed (feared?) each
had assigned to the other. Misunderstanding at almost every turn.
Failed struggle for "recognition."

I know: all these words will not prevent things from slipping away, but I will
write them, nonetheless.

When I awoke this morning, a memory of K. telling me, as he was peeing, that
his penis had grown during the night, "while my been sweeping."

The man with the long white beard walks so fast that it parts in the middle, each
half pushed over a shoulder by the air into which he is striding so
determinedly.

The influence of T.K.: after his rhapsodizing about yodelling, I begin to hear it,
softly, in everyone's speech.

Slipping her shoes off under the table, her toes tell her of freedom.

This word means: *the kind of memory that makes one feel lighter.*

Fantasy: at the rear of the church, in the middle of the *Credo*, a group of people
stand and sing the sauciest bits of the *Carmina Burana*. Not all of them
are naked.

I had to try hard to resist the temptation to ask the young museum attendant
what she really thought about the nudes of Schiele in the company of
which she spent every working day.

She sits herself down on a bench in the Burggarten as if she is waiting for the proper light—the real light—to find her and reveal her true beauty.

It's happened sooner than I had expected: my thoughts tumble and bump into each other in a jumble of languages. I am a Babel of inner dialogues.

The old man in the National Library: tenderly he places his aged hand on the page of the book—as once he must have placed his youthful hand on the cheek of his beloved.

This word means: *the pain a word encloses.*

After talking on the phone with S., I always remember something I wanted to tell her but that our conversation would not admit. How quickly and perfectly memory fails. There is never a shortage of the forgotten; never a shortage of separations.

I felt I was not being attentive enough to everything A. was trying to say, even as I felt that the attention the situation demanded was beyond my powers. At the table in the busy restaurant, a glass of fine white wine before me and all the elements of a memorable evening assembled, I felt doubly condemned.

He walks down the street as if he is in a hurry to fulfil an appointment with a mirror—but only the "right" mirror will do.

Ask any pair of lovers and they will tell you: street corners are provided so that there they may pause on their walks and kiss each other long and deep. This city, too, has a map of tenderness and love laid over it. For those who can see them, the streets are replete with "Kissing Stations."

She emerges from the building into the street with such a sigh and a curious smile—as if a secret door has opened before her and she is preparing to follow the advice that the kindly, bespectacled doctor has just given her: to dare to step through it before it closes forever.

While her dog was shitting on the grass, the teenaged girl closed her eyes and swayed her hips from side to side quite provocatively, as if she were alone and unseen in her bedroom at night.

The young woman walking down the street was holding in front of her face a GPS device that I took to be a compact mirror. When I realized my error, I was a bit disappointed. The thought of a person walking down the street while looking into a mirror appeals to me far more than that of a person consulting a GPS device.

When one leaves an art museum where one has been losing oneself for hours in the irreality of art, it is the "real world" that quickly assumes the quality of irreality. At the museum's exit, a sign should be posted: "Danger: Reality Starts Here."

It is not that I notice more in this unfamiliar place; it is simply that, in the wish to preserve a mutual unfamiliarity, I "authorize" myself to notice everything and muse with it.

> "For the quiet happiness of breathing, being able
> to be alive, tell me to whom I should be grateful."
> (Mandelshtam)

The teenaged couple in their school uniforms sitting silently on the park bench and staring into the near distance: are they joined by disparate thoughts? Or separated by a single thought?

> «There the stone is not dead.
> The wick flares
> When a glance ignites it»
> ("The Native Land")

52

One could view these football players and their games as resembling graceful dancers in a kind of ballet of combat; equally, if one is aware of the astronomical salaries the players receive, one could see them merely as money in motion; or, one can see them as both at once and order another beer.

Not only the "flow" of thoughts, but their "arrest" as well (Benjamin): my mode of composition.

The involuntary confession of the flowers in the vase.

The most effective way to neutralize an image consists in calling it "art."

The young woman working in the art gallery: her glowing bronze tan speaks of Mediterranean holidays, days on the beaches of Greek isles, etc.— speaks, then, of money. On the other hand, it may also speak of hours spent lying on a tanning bed. In which case, it speaks just as fluently of a certain poverty.

This word means: *the silence the music has made.*

The best known and most widely promoted of Schiele's paintings and drawings retain their provocative power because they confront the viewer with a fantasy of complete sexual availability. Terms such as "voluptuous lassitude," "decadent," "degenerate," and especially "libertinage" fail to do justice the works' ambiguities where a certain "creepiness," a mixture of fascination and aversion, can be felt. Schiele uncovers something even darker in the mythology of Love-Death. He uncovers the fact that the promise of complete sexual availability, while it suggests endless pleasures, an erotic Utopia aimed against the hypocritical morality of his own time, is also the promise of the very opposite of freedom.

The pigeon flew up to the window, stood on the ledge, and peered through the window as if looking for someone behind the glass from whom it could request a small loan. Finding no one there, it flew away *dejectedly*.

As I was reading, it was not the words I could not understand; rather, the *letters* of each word made no sense at all to me.

I've noticed that I am trying to make as little noise as possible when I walk through the flat, often on tiptoe. Perhaps I am practising to be a ghost.

"Adventures in attention."

I think today of the young couple sitting side-by-side in the restaurant a few nights ago and recall that I had to force myself not to stare at them. They were becoming even more beautiful with each adoring look they gave each other. —Beauty with a future.

The commonplace gesture of a man slapping another man on the back by way of greeting can open a crack in the veneer of a society's ways of appearing.

When the musicians have left the stage, no one pays any attention to the technicians as they go about their work—except other technicians.

«You must not cry,
says the music.

Otherwise
no one
says
anything.»
("Enigma")

All that fussing with her dress—pinching it together so that the breezes will
   not open its flaps, pulling it higher because it's strapless and threatens
   to expose her breasts with almost every move she makes—is not
   performed out of modesty but from nerves. She has not yet learned
   to permit and control all the viewer will *see*. She has not yet mastered
   the art of being looked at. Lacking this ability is commonly referred
   to as "innocence," a noun that, when deployed in this manner, can be
   followed through the entire range of moral and cultural values and
   their histories.

After a day in which, despite all my efforts, I accomplished very little (but I
   managed to find a stuffed doll for K.), I feel I have entered a very
   narrow part of myself. Perhaps the darkness, when it comes, will
   provide an opening.

I could not help but think it was a "lurid" kiss, but the look of the elderly woman
   next to the couple engaged in it went far beyond my impressions, for
   she was, with bobbing head upraised, studying every movement of the
   mouths and tongues with the curiosity and detachment that her age
   had conferred on her as a *right*. —A free-lance inspector of kisses, she.
   Her identity papers read: "Widow, Mother, Grandmother, Inspector of
   Kisses."

Two English-speaking teenaged boys, as they passed me this afternoon on
   Margaretenstraße:
   Boy 1: "Do you really think she'll be there?"
   Boy 2: "She'll be there, naked and willing."
   Boy 1: "Yes. Oh, yes. I will. Yes."
   How did so many of Molly Bloom's words get into this adolescent
   male's mouth?

I could not be the right person for that conversation. This realization, coming
   now, so long after the event, disarms me.

«Forever and No Longer mixed in a single drink.»
("Letter in Two Drafts")

This word means: *the absence of the sounds the children made when they were playing here.*

She sits down at the table as one who is content to be without any emotion whatever.

Walking back to the flat with the stuffed Einstein doll under my arm, I am almost elated until I imagine K.'s disappointment that I have not brought him a collection of tiny metal cars. By the time I climb the stairs and turn the key in the lock, I am quite forlorn.

This word means: *the bruise on a voice.*

Of the many severe tests that the dominant concepts of ethics must bear today, one of the most common must surely be an encounter with a beggar. That the concepts of "dignity," "respect," "responsibility," and "dialogue" all fail miserably should not go unnoticed and unconsidered, especially by those who espouse them. Likewise the notion of Christian charity, *Agape*, once considered a duty. (Because of its dutiful character, *Agape* possesses, or is held to possess, a dignity to which *Eros* cannot lay claim.) Today, if that "duty" is performed at all, it is done across a distance by a cheque written to an Agency (with a tax-deductible receipt in return); otherwise it is seen as an undertaking belonging to the offices of the state. In truth, the concrete *reality* of the beggar offends against the evocations of abstract "dignity," "responsibility," "respect," and "dialogue." The presupposition for the setting into action of these concepts is a condition of freedom and equality, neither of which the beggar, in a state of abject need, can satisfactorily claim. Because those from whom he or she seeks alms consider themselves to be the norm of humanity, the beggar standing before them in a state of need and destitution, must be (so the logic goes), the embodiment of the Less-Than-Human, an anomaly and an anachronism. That the beggar rejects, or finds impossible, such a "norm" calls into question everything on which that norm bases itself. The beggar exhibiting to the uninterested and the indifferent the sores, the amputated limbs, the babies asleep at the withered breast, the bent back, the missing teeth, knows more—and says more wordlessly— about the so-called "values" of "society" than any of its insiders can ever hope to know.

«And yet we want to speak across borders,
even if borders go right through every word.»
("Of a Land, a River and Lakes")

14.

At 5.30 a.m., the white-haired old lady who lives on the other side of Kühnplatz
is cooing and throwing crumbs from her window to the pigeons on
the ledge. After decades of rising early to cook and feed breakfast to
her family, she now lives alone, and her morning maternal duties are
directed to the birds that receive them with quiet appreciation. She has
made this new morning gentle with her care.

A bottle just fell over onto the street. It didn't break but only rolled for a while,
clinkety-clinkety-clinkety, until it stopped. The morning is still enough
to hear that.

Every morning: a new light to learn; every night: a star and its shadow.

An old woman sat for a while on a bench in the morning sunlight, her hands
lying in her lap as if they were small sleeping pets.

Some days: it's as if I must learn this language all over again. I could console
myself by thinking that I need these tests, these trials, these failures—
but I wouldn't believe it for a minute.

"Do Not Disturb: In this room objects are dreaming."

Everyone, even the proper looking gentleman who has just seated himself at a
table at the café-terrace's edge, has a part to play in the dramas enacted
here. His role is that of *The Observer*.

Another of B.'s comments that had the force of truth: that Ingeborg Bachmann
attempted to make herself into a work of art—that she was the artist
and the work "simultaneously." It is the word "simultaneously" that
makes all the difference.

I have not seen A. since our failed conversation of two nights ago, and I don't
think I will see her again before I have to return. I don't think either of
us has the intelligence or the courage to correct what we could not do.
And now the time to learn such intelligence and such courage as was
needed then has passed.

Sharing my bed: four books. "We take to bed lovers and books," Benjamin once
wrote. Oh, well, that's all I know.

"*La poesie, c'est d'etre absolument soi-même.*" (Verlaine?)

When a long pause in the conversation brought it to a halt ("*Une ange passé*")
that threatened to be its end, the thought occurred to me that the
others at the table were all thinking that they would prefer to be
somewhere else—perhaps because I would have preferred to be
somewhere else. Then we all looked at each other with a kind of guilty
silence in which could be observed the admission in our eyes that we'd
all had exactly the same thought.

The separation from S. and K. is most acutely felt when I am on the move. I want
to say to him, "Oh, look …" when I see the caryatids on the buildings,
the sunlight on the Danube, the many statues. I sometimes reach for
the touch of his little hand as I stroll along the streets, imagine him
running and running in the Prater. As S. and I would chat at a café
table in the late afternoon sunlight, he would colour pictures with
his crayons. Then, on our way back to the flat, the merchants in the
Naschmarkt, where we will have gone to get vegetables and fruit,
would make a big fuss over him and give him cherries and strawberries
and sweets.

I have often caught myself in silent dialogue with them, my distant
loves. My daily prayers.

«How shall I name myself,
without being in another language?»
("How Shall I Name Myself?")

When a weak darkness entered the room, I went to the window where I looked
out on a vast grey cloud looming in the sky. Then I saw that it was
moving very slowly and that its "uniform" grey actually contained blue,
white, and yellow and that its grey actually had different densities of
light and dark, mingling, swirling, and separating within it.

(The most wondrous moment in the film *The Girl With the Pearl
Earring*: when Grete, with quiet wonder, names to Vermeer the colours
the sky contains.)

The woman taking photographs in the street: as she aims her camera, she places
her left leg forward, adopting the position of the fencer's "*En garde!*"

This word means: *the language in which leaves whisper together.*

Standing outside the building where Auden died, I almost had a poem.

The child asks, "Do you want me to teach you how to watch?"

All Vienna tobacco shops have something of a sepulchral feel. Even when they
are not dark, they are dark; even when they are not narrow, they are
narrow; even when they are not cool, they are cool. The tobacco shops
are better reminders of mortality than all the government health
warnings that come on the products they sell.

The recollection of childhood moments does not only require solitude; it
produces solitudes.

When the woman server at the café where I have paused for an hour or so
almost every day for nearly a month greeted me this morning with
the customary "*Grüß Gott*" ("Greetings to God"), I returned her
salutation, but, knowing I was violating a principle of Viennese
etiquette, I inquired after her well-being. "How are you," I asked.
She smiled demurely and did not answer the question we both
knew I should not have asked. That I had asked it branded me as

a "stranger." That she had received it with a smile branded me as a "friendly stranger"—which is, after all, the truth. In any case, we shared a moment of amusement at the custom of maintaining a "polite distance" from functionaries and at the unspoken taboo against breaking it. Later, when I had paid the bill and rose from the table to go, she called out, "See you again!" and laughed. I did, too.

This word means: *the calm of the window.*

All the while they sat at the table talking and drinking white wine while their daughter, kneeling on the chair, drew pictures, her bare toes climbed and descended his leg inside his trousers. Their complicity in mutual flirtation and seduction: each wears the smile of simultaneous Yes-and-No. The woman, the man, and their child, each so full of attention. Unnoticed, magic is making itself. Here it is, for all to see: happiness.

Today I am made of the sound of rustling—and of the listening to it.

Reverie gives to the past a future, its proper future, for reveries know the past in all its possibilities.

While their little children are playing, many of the young mothers sit on the benches surrounding the small playground and quietly daydream—to judge by the faraway look on their tranquil faces. For these brief but peaceful reveries they may one day be grateful to their children.

"…those summers of another century…."—I read that phrase this morning, and it has accompanied me all day.

"He woke at 4.00 a.m. and, unable to return to sleep, he rose, made coffee, and drank a cup at the open window, looking down at the few drunks staggering along the quiet street. He turned his face to the first clearing of the sky, and closed his eyes, listening to the scattered birdsong rising on the approaching light. A feeling of serenity, at last, mixed with expectation. Impulsively, he decided he would go for a walk. He dressed himself quickly and let himself out quietly, flinching at the loud metallic echo of the sound of the bolt shooting into the lock. He walked slowly and quietly down the five flights of marble stairs, across the foyer to the door, opened it, and stepped out. The cool air of a morning not yet officially begun greeted his face. On the street, a delivery van passed. He passed an old man walking his dog. On the Rechte Wienzeile at that hour there was no traffic at all. The stalls at the Naschmarkt were full of emptiness and stillness. In two hours or less, the vendors would arrive and begin setting up. In three hours, the first customers would appear. In four hours, the market would be busy and rich with its commotion of bodies and voices, colours and aromas; from its every corner, a living noise of desires, of asking and receiving, selling and buying, would hover in the atmosphere until sundown. But for this brief time a deep quiet owned the place. A cat, followed by another, darted unheard between stalls. A woman's high-heeled shoes tapped a brisk rhythm on the pavement. The first rays of sunlight were touching the tops of buildings opposite. Then he heard a low rumbling growing in the distance. It grew louder, as if approaching, slowly, very slowly but very steadily, the rumbling now louder, but as if inside a constant clanking, and grinding. He closed his eyes and stood stock-still, his whole body listening. The sound grew louder; it was coming his way. When he opened his eyes again, he saw them, the barrels of their big guns moving through shafts of sunlight and shade: the tanks had arrived…."

K.'s little voice in my ears: my morning's music.

At what point in a relationship do lovers cease to sit side-by-side and begin to sit face-to-face? The two lovers I saw in the restaurant the other night have not reached that point. —And I hope they never will.

"Here you will be the only noise, even if you do not say a word."

«Nothing more beautiful under the sun than to be under the sun»
("To the Sun")

62

This word means: *a rose-coloured whisper.*

Repetition, unremitting repetition, is the life, the death, and perhaps even the consolation of pornography. So, too, of sports—and so, too, of sports fans. "Sports porn."

> «[Y]our heart is busy elsewhere,
> your mouth takes in new tongues.»
> ("Tell Me, Love")

My unshakable ambivalence toward any event called a "festival" (of sport, of music, of theatre, of dance, etc.). When I am at a "festival," I am always mindful of its "unfestive" elements, the bureaucratic planning of it, the organization of it, the logistics of staging it, the people for whom it is a time and a place of work. The line dividing the "work" from the "enjoyment" or the "merriment" is, in most cases, a blurred one. For, while it is undeniable that the behaviours of the workers have been submitted to through calculation by those in charge, it is equally undeniable that the presence and behaviours of the attendees have been likewise calculated with the purpose of eliminating, as thoroughly as possible, the element of chance. Hence, the organized, even regimented, behaviour of those who attend a festival is as plainly discernible as the placement of seats, the location of the stages, the corridors that have been erected to regulate pedestrian traffic— though, in the "spirit of festivity," no one is supposed to perceive it. Moreover, because the "spirit of festivity" presides as the *prima causa*, pleasure, permitted only the semblance of spontaneity, is obligatory. Spontaneity has narrow limits to which it must give obedience. "Festivals" are not very unlike Sade's orgies: planned, designed, and stage-managed in almost every detail.

This city carries on an unending and noisy architectural argument with itself— but *sotto voce.*

This word means: *the sound of a footstep lifted from the pavement.*

"When I get too tired, I talk too much—or not at all."

He walks down the street in a manner reminiscent of a boxer walking to the ring where victory or defeat awaits him: his every movement in accord with a music that no one but he can hear.

Airports await us, knowingly, smugly, in all the languages of the world.

The large-sized sigh that escaped me as I ambled through the Naschmarkt eating a Lebanese pistachio-stuffed cookie—the breath of my happiness and its absence at once.

As the market was preparing to close, the man at one of the vegetable stalls lifted his T-shirt and exuberantly rubbed his big, hairy belly. Perhaps financiers, government ministers, bureaucrats, doctors, and lawyers should do the same at the end of their workday.

Perhaps the child is about to discover a new emotion at the precise moment when its mother might convince herself that the supply of emotion has been completely exhausted.

This word means: *all the rain hears in its falling.*

The exultant cry of victory (at the scoring of a goal or at a goalie's save) has its roots in the howl of grief and despair that it seeks to overpower and drown.

She raised her hand slowly to her mouth and touched her fingers to her lips as if recounting, one at a time, some of the places where they had been.

15

"Drenched in history"... "bathed in history"... "soaked in history"... "saturated
   with history"—all of which mean, of course, decay.

My habit of lodging pens and pencils in the books I am reading.

"He may be misanthropic, but that's not the point. Besides, misanthropy has
   much to recommend it." (Fragment of a conversation overheard last
   night in the *Museums Quartier*)

Trying to assemble from my meagre provisions something I could make for
   dinner, I became so tired and confused that I had to lie down.

They speak German, but they laugh in their native language.

The *form* of an emotion, the *form* of a thought—ah, but now we are talking
   about art.

The two policemen watching the performers at the *Straßenfest*—they applaud so
   loudly and so heartily at the conclusion of every number that I cannot
   help but wonder if they are recent graduates of a Police Department
   PR course.

The children are not interested in the music or the musicians; they are interested
   in their game and in each other. Such intensity and concentration.
   They have not yet been drilled by distractions.

The park: a public shelter for reveries—the place where reverie's history can be
   entered through any gate, traced along any path.

The young woman with the child in her arms enters the playground as if it were hostile territory. —And, judging from the way the small girl is clinging to her mother, she seems to think so, too.

The band played "The Tennessee Waltz." They followed it (as I had guessed they would—and it was a wild guess) with "Until The Next Teardrop Falls." When they finished, loud calls of *"Encore!"*—as if everyone had guessed wildly and correctly.

Now (7.30 p.m.) the sunlight is coming through the east windows again— reflected from the apartments on the other side of the *Platz* that face west.

All the people eating and drinking at tables in the street while facing a very large television screen from which images and commentary are aimed at them: is this a variation on the 1950s "TV Dinner" eaten by the gathered family on its "TV tables?" Or is it a variation, *mit Gemütlichkeit,* on Orwell's *1984?*

The thought, as I pass them, that these old buildings are keeping to themselves and guarding centuries-old secrets that no one will ever know or disclose.

"What is behind that door?" he asked. "The Room of Angers," she replied.

"Farrago"—a word I've too long ignored.

Because I slept until 5.15 this morning, I feel I can face any coming catastrophe—no anxieties or jitters.

At dawn, with their arms draped around each other, they danced a slow waltz
down the sleeping street.

"J'ai embrassé l'aube d'èté.

Man to Police Officer: "I'm not drunk. My motorcycle is drunk."

The child moves through the book of fairy stories with a peculiar alertness to
what looms in the dark forests, to the crumbs left on the path, to the
ladder of the beanstalk. Something similar is true of the adult who
moves through the city of Vienna as if through a scrapbook.

"I have a talent for silence. Who, today, could say that? I know the kinds of
storms one silence can contain."

In the warm weather, clothes have come off, and tattoos have come out.

"We did not find the Museum of Historical Sorrows, but we found the sounds of
sighs and weeping that were hanging in the trees."

I began to suspect that she speaks so often of "kindness," "respect," and "giving
encouragement," etc. because she wants to believe that, in her maturity,
she is above the wrongs she committed in her youth. The wrongs she
now commits are made of pious platitudes and sanctimonious self-
contentment.

The clouds here have not been "burned off" by the sun or blown away by the
wind: they have moved into me.

Time to go out and make a new noise.

Thinking around a corner.

There is no window that does not see her.

The flat seemed more cheerful when I opened the door and heard Bach's *Partitas for Violin*. I thought for a moment that someone had come in when I was at the market and sat listening to them while waiting for me to return.

This word means: *the sound sunlight makes on the top of a cloud.*

The tattoos the Viennese wear are like those worn in the U.S. and Canada, and they wear them on identical places of their anatomy. There don't appear to me specifically Viennese, or Austrian tattoos. Perhaps we should be thankful for that. A specifically Viennese or Austrian tattoo might be very frightening to behold.

Father to child: "You have been a very naughty boy, so now you must go the Office of the Admonisher."

Beneath the table, their knees are considering each other.

With his "team" of employees, the owner of the Sekt Comptoir across the street is preparing for the *Straßenfest*, which begins at 1.00 p.m. today. It is not yet 10.00, and he is sipping from his product as he supervises the workers. —A "hair of the dog?" or the wings of an angel?

The shadow of an airplane just glided through the room.

"It's perfectly acceptable to sit in your underwear at the table. Once, in a movie, I saw John Travolta, wearing only his underwear, sitting at a table. But he was eating breakfast. He wasn't writing in a book and occasionally looking out the window, as you are doing."

Just to see people in conversation: the gestures, the movements of body and
eyes—all in service to the mouth, the words. All of it so sensual.

In all the creases and wrinkles of its ruination, his face preserves the face of the
child he once was. It is a sunny and breezy Thursday afternoon in
Vienna, June 2008, as he hands me a leaflet advertising a sale in one
of the larger stores on Kärtnerstraße, but the smile he bestows to one
and all has travelled the distance from his true un-time and un-place:
Judgement Day.

16.

Trances of morning's light.

> "Listen. Daddy is killing Mommy."
> "No he isn't. He loves Mommy."
> "Then what's that noise she's making?"
> "I don't know. (Pause.) What's that?"
> "Now Mommy is killing Daddy. They're killing each other."
> "Maybe they're just fighting again."
> "No, I don't think so."
> "Listen."
> "I can't hear anything."
> "Me either."
> "Do you think they're dead?"
> "No, they're breathing and whispering. Can you hear it?
> "They're breathing awfully fast. What are they whispering?"
> "I don't know. I can't make it out."
> "Is it good or bad?
> "It's good, I think."

On the floor by my suitcase I've assembled all the trophies and gifts I will bring back. Travellers are expected to return with "booty" to distribute and stories to tell.

> Q: Why did you come to Vienna?
> A: To find time.
> Q: Oh. And did you find the time you were looking for?
> A: No, I lost time.
> Q: Perhaps they are the same.

I've begun to talk to myself in English again.

Suddenly, everywhere I look are people wearing baseball caps backwards and carrying bottles of water. Now I know it's time to go.

The road—any road— to Utopia is paved with the trash of destroyed hopes.

17.

Six in the morning: Bach, birds, and me.

The sound of the woman coughing in the apartment below.

I know nouns—many—that do not deserve to begin with a capital letter.

When I looked out the window a moment ago to see how the morning was
shaping up, the street below was completely empty. But suddenly
people entered it from all directions at once, as if it were a movie set
and the order "Action!" had just been given.

As I listened to her speaking yesterday at the table, the bustle and the noise of
the festival surrounding, I had the feeling that her body and her soul
were hanging on her voice.

This word means: *the shape of an absence now occupying the chair.*

Opening and closing the shades according to the direction and passage of the
sunlight into the rooms.

"...at odds with the obedient world."
(Mandelshtam)

"When he had what he considered to be a good thought, he rewarded himself
with a drink of wine. The drink of wine rewarded him with another
good thought, which, in turn, was rewarded with another sip of
wine...."

This word means: *the sound of a breath falling to the floor in an empty room.*

Q: And what exactly did you accomplish in Vienna?
A: I walked around, looked around, listened around, and I wrote.
Q: Yes? And what did you write? Stories? Poems? Dramas?
A: I wrote what could be thought to be little stories with little dramas
       in them.
Q: And these little "stories," as you call them, did you make them up or
       are they based on life?
A: I wrote stories of life making up stories.
Q: I see. You have gathered evidence.
A: Yes.

"The man who returns from afar lies with impunity," wrote Gaston Bachelard—
       and such a lie might very well be one of the oldest and deepest sources
       of story-telling. With the first words of the lie, the story has begun. By
       the time it has reached its end, that lie will have uncovered truths both
       shallow and profound.

"Daddy, everything is magic."

      «In an arrogant age
      one must flee from one light
      into another. . .»
      ("Curriculum Vitae")

Afterword

The fragments presented in the foregoing pages testify unashamedly to a concern with the particularities of experience, a concern which entails that the customary boundary-line between what is referred to as "philosophy" and what is referred to as "poetry" necessarily becomes porous. The product of their reciprocal interpenetrations signals nothing less than a certain identity-less-ness as a condition of freedom. If philosophy conceives of this freedom in terms of "Utopia," poetry perceives its "No-Man's-Land" to be the true place of human habitation. The enduring qualities that thought confers upon Utopia are first learned in its encounters with all that is fleeting, transitory, fortuitous. The *as if* which poetry exercises, the imagining of things otherwise with which all utopian thought is tasked, is not incompatible with that particular form of astonishment that is indissociable from an extreme attention to what is.

These pieces were written in June 2008 in Vienna where I had traveled to pursue research into the works of one of this world's great writers, Ingeborg Bachmann. That her many and varied writings (they include lyric poetry, short stories, radio dramas, opera libretti, public lectures, essays, and novels) remain so little known in North America, despite many very capable English-language versions, is truly a terrible shame. Her poems, breathed aloud, in the almost whispered way I once heard her give voice to them on a late night radio broadcast, accompanied me day and night. In Vienna, as once long ago when I was a young man in Vancouver, these poems found me when, though I did not know it, I needed them. My translations of lines from her poems and from an early prose work appear here in *guillemets* («...»). They are as faithful to her thought and to her prosody as I could make them, though I do not pretend to any literariness. The lines from Osip Mandelshtam are translated from Paul Celan's German translation of that great Russian poet. Even when the fragments presented here are not themselves translations, translation itself is often their true source. That can mean, especially, the carrying over in words one form of silence, with whatever it may contain of attention, solitude, destitution, freedom, imagination, and/or memory, to another form of silence. Walter Benjamin once referred to writings of Karl Kraus (from whom the epigraph to this work is taken) as "a silence turned inside out." With those words he may very well have given the truest definition to all that which goes by the name "writing."

· · · ·

A word should be said about some of the physical, material places named in these pages, for all is not words. Bordered on its north by the busy traffic artery Linke Wienzeile and on its south by the equally busy Rechte

Wienzeile, the Naschmarkt, Vienna's largest outdoor market, contains many different kinds of eateries, drinkeries, and all the foodstuffs that could satisfy even the most demanding culinary requirements. It is bisected by Schleifmühlgasse. On Saturdays, its extreme end is occupied by a gigantic Flea Market. Margaretenstraße turns into the Operngasse, leading directly to the Opera House (Staatsoper). Wiedener Hauptstraße, where it meets the Opera, becomes Kärtnersrtaße, one of the wide pedestrian shopping streets in the city, lined with many shops of all kinds. It leads directly to St Stephan's Church (Stephansdom) and the Graben, another broad pedestrian thoroughfare given over to all manner of shops and commerce. Along these streets, one can enounter a diversity of architectural styles, from the Baroque to Jugendstil to the modern. Mariahilferstraße is also a commercial street, containing many shops, chain stores, chain coffee shops, etc. In addition to these, there are, however, a number of surviving and thriving older cafés and, in the neighbouring streets, ethnic shops, markets, restaurants, clubs, and cultural centres. The Museumsquartier, a kind of post-modern cultural theme park, consists of museums, galleries, cafés, etc. The Albertina once housed apartments for visitors to the imperial court; now it houses one of the largest collections of graphic art in the world. From its rampart one can see, across Albertinaplatz, the Café Mozart, located behind the Staatsoper. The story told of the "Aryanization" of the Café Mozart is true. The Café Sperl permits no cell phones within its walls. There one can be safely and securely "out of touch"—if only for a little while.

. . . .

I extend my thanks to Queen's University and to the Queen's University Faculty Association for awarding me a grant that made travel to Vienna and living there possible. I also express deep gratitude to Ines Rieder who, with the grace and generosity that is so characteristic of her, made her flat and her city available to me. All who have ever gathered together around her table know themselves to be fortunate, indeed. I continue to converse with Robert Adrian, Heidi Grundmann, and Tomás Kalmar, if only, during times of interruption, with inward voice. The presence of Helen Humphreys in this world makes it a truly better place.